DO MY HAIR LIKE THAT!

A collection of hair inspirations for black and brown girls & the people who style their hair.

CREATED BY:

Victoria McKnight

DESIGNED BY:

KoS Design Inc

COPYRIGHT PAGE

For Camille; My pure inspiration.
You are my reason to evolve, experiment, and grow.
You are love.

Contents:

İNTRODUCTION:

Time to do my little one's hair! Just the sound of the water in the tub freaked her out!

But I kept my cool! I showed her a picture-grid of little-girl hairstyles and said "Which hairstyle do you want, baby?" Camille looked, smiled, and chose a style. Children love choices.

After that, I was able to coax, laugh, hug, and patiently comb her hair into some really great designs.

So our hair journey strengthened. Every time it was time to wash and get her hair done, I brought out that picture grid. She loved that we had done this one or that one, and her excitement and the ease of deciding how to do her hair, was my inspiration behind this book.

@koily_kali

@koily_kali

@koily_kali

@koily_kali

@ kyra_milan

@kyra_milan

@kyra_milan

@kyra_milan

@kyra_milan

@kyra_milan

1

2

@kyra_milan

3

4

@kyra_milan

13

14

20

Slow down a bit:
Multiple Techniques

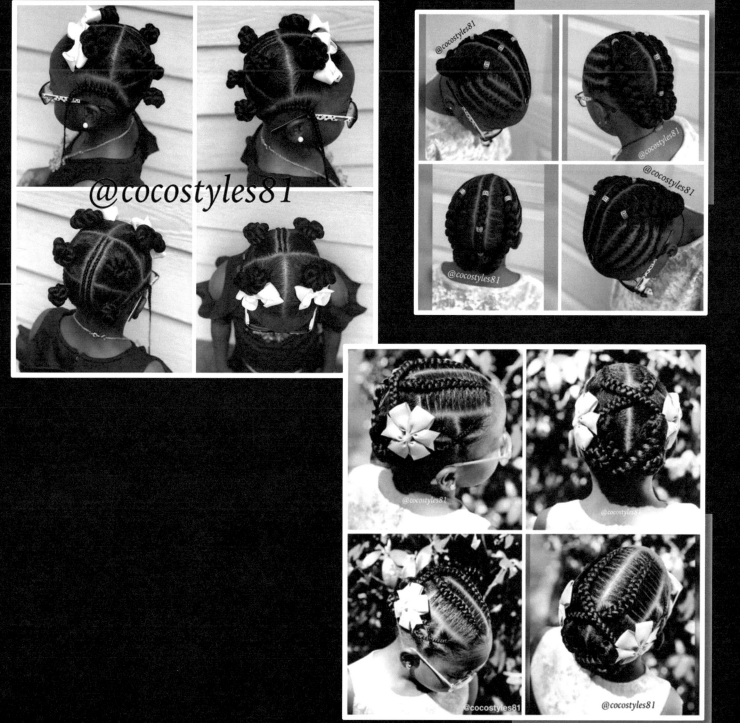

@cocostyleshair

The Natural Hair Studio NJ

The Natural Hair Studio NJ

The Natural Hair Studio NJ

The Natural Hair Studio NJ

The Natural Hair Studio NJ

The Natural Hair Studio NJ

The Natural Hair Studio NJ

The Natural Hair Studio NJ

CAUTION

HIRE A PROFESSIONAL!

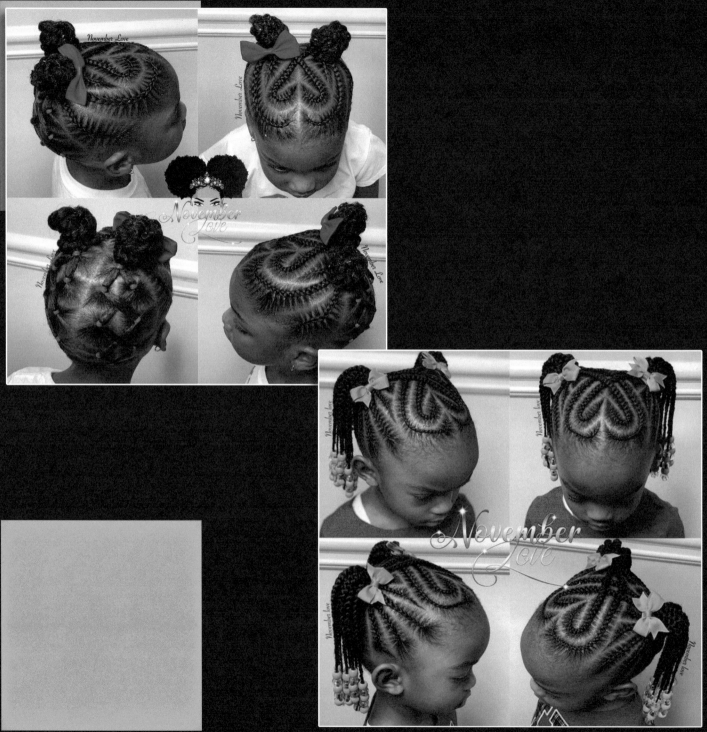

CREDITS

KYRA AND KALI

Kyra, 9yo
@kyra_milan

Kyra is an IG hair influencer with over 80,000 followers, and she has
an awesome hair tutorial channel on YouTube. Kyra and her sister
Kali are the faces of Koily Kurls; an online hair boutique with hair
essentials, tools, robes and even kitten heels!

Kali, 5yo
@koily_kali

This little natural beauty has over 7,000 followers on IG. Kali is such a
fun spirited little girl, and she loves her hair best when it's curled!

Kali wants to add cute backpacks to their online store!
This influencer loves beads, beads, and more beads!

Check out their online boutique!
www.koilykurls.com

KIA GARRET

@KiaBia87
Georgia, USA

Ms. Kia Garrett is an artist through and through!
Check out r IG @kiabia87

Hair Tip:
Low manipulation!
"Let your hair be."

Shea Matthews

@HayvensHair
California, USA

Both of this stylist's parents are in the hair industry–so it isn't a coincidence that she showed talent very early on. Shea grew up with her hair "permed and pressed" and she began doing her own hair in middle school! Now she has a following of almost 30,000 people on IG who ask her for hair inspirations and tutorials!

Preferred Hair Tool:
Purple parting comb "It makes every style!"

Sharonda Andrews

@cocostyles81
Georgia, USA

This Atlanta stylist specializes in crochet, twists, and stitch braids. "I help natural women keep their hair healthy and their edges in place."

Check out www.cocostyleshair.com

Kayla White

@novemberlov3
Georgia, USA

This stylist has over 150,000 followers on IG! She's pushing the boundaries of hair braiding techniques!

Check out www.novemberlovebraids.com

Jennifer Cherilus

@thenaturalhairstudionj
New Jersey, USA

"Where we are unapologetically natural, and eager to share knowledge about natural hair care and styling!"

Check out www.thenaturalhairstudionj.com

Made in the USA
Columbia, SC
14 December 2024

49426985R00022